D1567626

HARVEST HOUSE PUBLISHERS
Eugene, Oregon

Dear Child of Mine

Eugene, Oregon 97402

ISBN 0-7369-0790-4

Design and production by Garborg Design Works, Minneapolis, Minnesota

Printed in Hong Kong.

02 03 04 05 06 07 08 09 10 11 / NG / 10 9 8 7 6 5 4 3 2 1

The experiences you have had are your own greatest treasure, well worth the remembering and retelling.

RAY MUNGO

Dear Child of Mine,

It is with a heart full of joy that I have kept this journal as a celebration of all the special memories you and I have shared. Let this be a keepsake of treasured moments in your life—people, places, and events that have made you the extraordinary person you are.

I pray that as you read these remembrances, your heart recognizes they were written in unconditional love—a mother's love. You are precious to me and I thank God He has blessed me with such a wonderful child.

From My Heart to Yours...

Our Family Tree
Mom
You
Dad

Like branches on a tree, we may grow in different directions,

Yet our roots remain as one.

Each of our lives will always be a special part of the other.

Your Maternal Grandparents

Grandma's maiden name:

Her birthday:

Grandma was born in:

Grandpa's name:

His birthday:

Grandpa was born in:

PLACE PHOTO HERE

Here are some of Grandma's favorite childhood memories:

Here are some of Grandpa's favorite childhood memories:

Train up a child in the way he should go, and when he is old, he will not depart from it.

THE BOOK OF PROVERBS

How Grandma and Grandpa met:

They were married:

Their favorite things they like to do together:

Their children:

What I want you to know about your maternal grandparents:

How you remind me of them:

Grandma's Favorite Things

Color: ______________ Flower: ______________

Flavor of tea: ______________ Ice Cream/Dessert: ______________

Music: ______________

Book/Author: ______________

Movie/Actor: ______________

Things to do on a rainy day: ______________

____

Things to do on a sunny day: ______________

____

Vacation spot: ______________

Poem/Verse: ______________

____

Meal/Recipe: ______________

____

Other special stuff: ______________

____

____

____

Grandpa's Favorite Things

Color: ______________________ Hobby: ______________________

Sport: ______________________ Ice Cream/Dessert: ______________

Music: ____

Book/Author: ____

Movie/Actor: ____

Things to do on a rainy day: ___________________________

____

Things to do on a sunny day: ___________________________

____

Vacation spot: ______________________________

Poem/Verse: ______________________________

____

Meal/Recipe: ______________________________

____

Other special stuff: __________________________

____

____

____

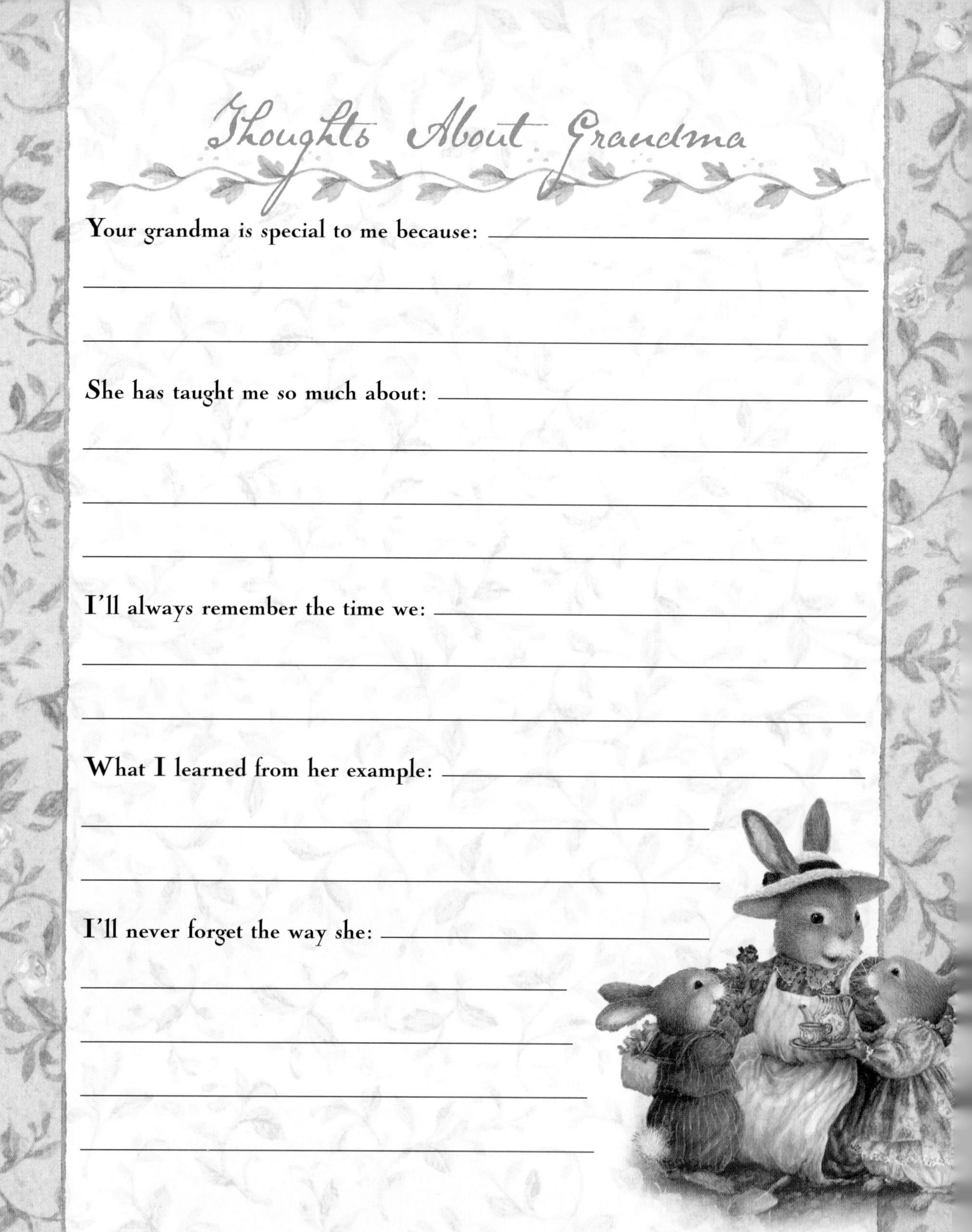

Thoughts About Grandma

Your grandma is special to me because: ____________________

____

____

She has taught me so much about: ____________________

____

____

____

I'll always remember the time we: ____________________

____

____

What I learned from her example: ____________________

____

____

I'll never forget the way she: ____________________

____

____

____

____

Thoughts About Grandpa

Your grandpa is special to me because: ______________________

____

____

He has taught me so much about: ______________________

____

____

____

I'll always remember the time we: ______________________

____

____

What I learned from his example: ______________________

____

____

I'll never forget the way he: ______________________

____

____

____

____

Your Paternal Grandparents

Grandma's maiden name:

Her birthday:

Grandma was born in:

Grandpa's name:

His birthday:

Grandpa was born in:

PLACE PHOTO
HERE

Here are some of Grandma's favorite childhood memories:

What greater thing is there for human souls than to feel that they are joined for life—to be with each other in silent unspeakable memories.

GEORGE ELIOT

Here are some of Grandpa's favorite childhood memories:

How Grandma and Grandpa met:

They were married:

Their favorite things they like to do together:

Their children:

What I want you to know about your paternal grandparents:

Youth fades, love droops,
the leaves of friendship fall;
A mother's secret hope
outlives them all.

OLIVER WENDELL HOLMES

How you remind me of them:

Grandma's Favorite Things

Color: ______________________ Flower: ______________________

Flavor of tea: ______________________ Ice Cream/Dessert: ______________________

Music: ____

Book/Author: ____

Movie/Actor: ____

Things to do on a rainy day: ____

____

Things to do on a sunny day: ______________________

____

Vacation spot: ______________________________

Poem/Verse: ______________________________

____

Meal/Recipe: ______________________________

____

Other special stuff: ____

____

____

____

Grandpa's Favorites Things

Color: ______________________ Hobby: ______________________

Sport: ______________________ Ice Cream/Dessert: ______________________

Music: ______________________

Book/Author: ______________________

Movie/Actor: ______________________

Things to do on a rainy day: ______________________

____

Things to do on a sunny day: ______________________

____

Vacation spot: ______________________

Poem/Verse: ______________________

____

Meal/Recipe: ______________________

____

Other special stuff: ______________________

____

____

____

Thoughts About Grandma

Your grandma is special to your dad because: ____________

____

____

She has taught him so much about: ____________

____

____

____

He'll always remember the time they: ____________

____

____

What he learned from her example: ____________

____

____

Your dad will never forget the way Grandma: ____________

____

____

____

____

Thoughts About Grandpa

Your grandpa is special to your dad because: ______________________

____

____

He has taught him so much about: ______________________

____

____

____

He'll always remember the time they: ______________________

____

____

What your dad learned from his example: ______________________

____

____

Your dad will never forget the way Grandpa: ______________________

____

____

____

____

PLACE PHOTO
HERE

My maiden name: ______

My birthday: ______

I was born in: ______

When I was young, people used to call me: ______

Some of my best childhood memories are: ______

______

______

______

My brothers and sisters are: ______

______

______

My favorite pet growing up was: ______

______

______

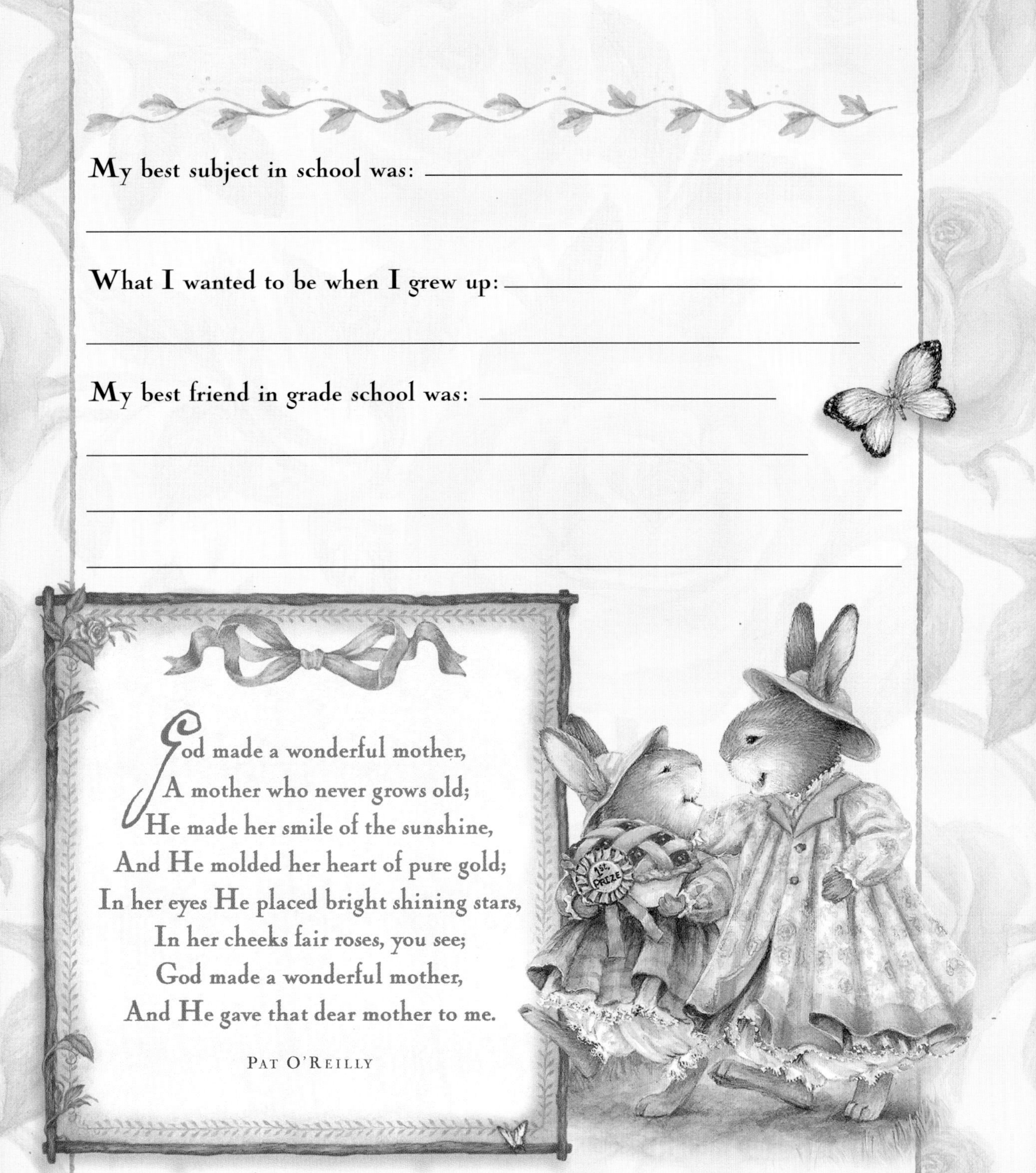

My best subject in school was: ______________________

____

What I wanted to be when I grew up: ______________________

____

My best friend in grade school was: ______________________

____

____

____

God made a wonderful mother,
A mother who never grows old;
He made her smile of the sunshine,
And He molded her heart of pure gold;
In her eyes He placed bright shining stars,
In her cheeks fair roses, you see;
God made a wonderful mother,
And He gave that dear mother to me.

PAT O'REILLY

I loved to eat: ______________________________

I enjoyed reading: ______________________________

Songs I remember best are: ______________________________

Television shows I never missed: ______________________________

The movies I liked to watch the most were: ______________________________

My favorite outfit was: ______________________________

On rainy days, I loved to: ______________________________

____

On sunny days, I loved to: ______________________________

____

My favorite toys I played with: ______________________________

People I looked up to: ______________________________

Best vacation: ______________________________

____

Other childhood favorites: ______________________________

____

____

____

Memories of my first date or dance:

The first time I fell in love:

Today's experiences are tomorrow's memories.

BARBARA JOHNSON

My best friend in high school was:

In high school, I was involved in:

My first job was: ______________________

____

____

The fashion craze was: ______________

____

World events: ____________________

____

____

After high school, I: ________________________

____

____

____

Other memories: ____

____

____

____

____

____

She is clothed with strength and dignity; she can laugh at the days to come. She speaks with wisdom, and faithful instruction is on her tongue. She watches over the affairs of her household and does not eat the bread of idleness. Her children arise and call her blessed.

THE BOOK OF PROVERBS

All About Dad

His birthday:

He was born in:

PLACE PHOTO HERE

When he was little, his nickname was:

Some of his best childhood memories are:

His brothers and sisters are:

His favorite pet growing up was:

His best subject in school was: ______________________________

What he wanted to be when he grew up: ______________________________

____

His best friend in grade school was: ______________________________

____

____

A father is many things to his child. As a teacher, he helps us learn valuable lessons...As a guide, he sets a pattern for life—for the ideals we should embrace and the goals we should seek. As a companion, he provides that close friendship God wishes for every young person to enjoy. It is, indeed, through the influence of a father on earth that we better know and understand our Father in heaven.

JAMES KELLER

Dad's Childhood Favorites

He loved to eat: ______________________________

He enjoyed reading: ______________________________

Sports he loved playing: ______________________________

Television shows he never missed: ______________________________

The movies he liked to watch the most were: ______________________________

His favorite T-shirt was: ______________________________

On rainy days, he loved to: ______________________________

____

On sunny days, he loved to: ______________________________

____

His favorite toys he played with: ______________________________

People he looked up to: ______________________________

Best vacation: ______________________________

____

Other childhood favorites: ______________________________

____

____

____

His Growing Up

Memories of his first date or dance: ______________

____

____

The first time he fell in love: ______________

____

____

His best friend in high school was: ______________

____

____

____

In high school, he was involved in: ______________

____

____

____

____

____

____

____

His first job was: ____________________

The fashion craze was: ____________________

World events: ____________________

After high school he: ____________________

Other memories: ____________________

From your parents you learn love and laughter and how to put one foot before the other.

HELEN HAYES

When I First Fell in Love with Your Dad

Your dad and I first met: ______________________________

____

____

My first impression of him: ______________________________

____

His first impression of me: ______________________________

____

Things we liked to do: ______________________________

____

____

____

How your dad proposed to me: ______________________________

____

____

The first people we told: ______________________________

____

____

We were married on: ____________________ at: ____________________

____________________ by: ____________________

Our bridal party included: ____________________

____

My favorite memory from the wedding is: ____________________

____

____

The funniest thing that happened on our wedding day: ____________________

____

____

Our honeymoon: ____________________

____

____

What I want you to know about marriage: ____________________

____

____

____

____

____

Love always protects,
always trusts, always hopes,
always perseveres.
Love never fails.

THE BOOK OF
1 CORINTHIANS

Your Parents, the Newlyweds

Our first home was: ____________________

____

As newlyweds, we spent a lot of time: ____________________

____

____

____

____

Our good friends at the time were: ____________________

____

____

Your dad worked at: ____________________

I worked at: ____________________

World events that affected us: ____________________

____

____

____

____

Our plans and dreams as a young couple:

Other thoughts about our early years:

The only gift is a portion of thyself.

RALPH WALDO EMERSON

My Favorite Things

Color: ______________________ Flower: ______________________

Flavor of tea: ______________________ Ice Cream/Dessert: ______________________

Music: ______________________

Book/Author: ______________________

Movie/Actor: ______________________

Things to do on a rainy day: ______________________

____

Things to do on a sunny day: ______________________

____

Vacation spot: ______________________

Poem/Verse: ______________________

____

Meal/Recipe: ______________________

____

Other special stuff: ______________________

____

____

____

Dad's Favorite Things

Color: ____________________ Hobby: ____________________

Sport: ____________________ Ice Cream/Dessert: ____________________

Music: ____________________

Book/Author: ____________________

Movie/Actor: ____________________

Things to do on a rainy day: ____________________

____

Things to do on a sunny day: ____________________

____

Vacation spot: ____________________

Poem/Verse: ____________________

____

Meal/Recipe: ____________________

____

Other special stuff: ____________________

____

____

____

Our Sweet Bundle of Love

The minute I learned you were coming, I: ______________________

____

____

____

When I told your dad, he: ______________________

____

____

____

To get ready for your arrival, we: ______________________

____

____

____

When I went into labor, your dad: ______________________

____

____

____

____

____

Children are the hands by which we take hold of heaven.

HENRY WARD BEECHER

You arrived at: ______________ on: ______________

at ______________________________ hospital.

When I first saw you, I: ______________

____

____

When your dad first saw you, he: ______________

____

____

The moment I first held you, I felt: ______________

____

A baby is God's opinion that life should go on.

CARL SANDBURG

Your name is special because: ______________

____

When the rest of the family heard about your arrival, they: ______________

____

Other fun memories: ______________

____

____

____

____

Love Notes from Mom

Love Notes from Dad

Lord I submit myself to you…Make me the parent You want me to be and teach me how to pray and truly intercede for the life of this child. I ask that you will increase my faith to believe for all the things You've put on my heart to pray for concerning this child.

STORMIE OMARTIAN

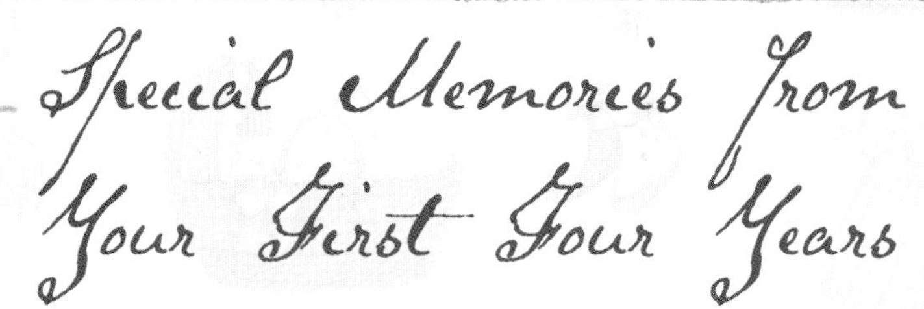

Special Memories from Your First Four Years

As a baby, you were: ____________________

You would only stop crying if we: ____________________

A toy you became very attached to: ____________________

The most surprising thing you did as a toddler was: ____________________

You made people laugh by: ______________________________

____

____

At bedtime, you: ______________________________

____

____

Your first gift to me: ______________________________

____

____

Some of my most precious memories of you as a toddler:

____

____

____

____

____

____

____

____

A happy childhood is one of the best gifts that parents have in their power to bestow.

R. CHOLMONDELEY

School Days

Your first school was: ______________________________

On your first day of school, I felt: ______________________________

____

____

Your first impressions of school were: ______________________________

____

Your teachers said: ______________________________

____

In grade school, you really liked: ______________________________

____

Your favorite teacher was: ______________________________

____

I'll never forget when you: ______________________________

____

Other fun memories: ______________________________

____

____

____

Give a little love to a child,
and you get a great deal back.

JOHN RUSKIN

Your Favorite Things

You loved to eat: ______________________________

Your favorite bedtime story: ______________________________

Song we used to sing together: ______________________________

Television shows you never missed: ______________________________

Movies you loved: ______________________________

You were always wearing: ______________________________

Things you liked to do on rainy days: ______________________________

____

Things you liked to do on sunny days: ______________________________

____

Your favorite toys: ______________________________

____

Places you liked to visit: ______________________________

A pet you really loved: ______________________________

Games and sports you played: ______________________________

Other fun favorites: ______________________________

____

____

Junior High Years

On your first day of junior high, I could tell: ______________________

Your attitude about school at the time was: ______________________

I enjoyed watching you excel in: ______________________

The day you became a teenager, I felt: ______________________

Our relationship changed in these ways: ______________________

What you thought you wanted to be when you grew up: ______________________

Some unforgettable memories from this time in your life: ______________________

Your Circle of Friends

Your first "best friend" was: ______________________

____

Close friends of yours that I really enjoyed: ______________________

____

____

You and your friends loved to: ______________________

____

____

____

I think you make a good friend because: ______________________

____

____

____

____

____

____

____

____

Pathway of Promise

The one thing I remember most about your high school years is: __________

I enjoyed watching you be involved in: __________

I was so proud of you when: __________

The first time you earned your own money, I knew: __________

The day you got your driver's license, I: __________

We can't form our children on our own concepts; we must take them and love them as God gives them to us.

GOETHE

I remember your first date: ______________________

____

____

When you had your first heartbreak, I: ______________________

____

____

After high school, you planned to: ______________________

____

On your graduation day, I felt: ______________________

____

____

Our relationship during that time was: ______________________

____

____

More memorable moments: ______________________

____

____

____

____

Our Family

In our family, you are always the one who: ______________________

What makes you different from your siblings: ______________________

How you're like me: ______________________

How you're like your dad: ______________________

Good family life is never an accident but always an achievement by those who share it.

JAMES BOSSARD

There's a family resemblance between you and:

What we appreciate most about you:

Family times I'll always remember:

Special Family Traditions and Celebrations

Your favorite holiday has always been: ____________________

____

Our most important family tradition to me is: ____________________

____

____

____

____

Precious holiday memories: ____________________

____

____

____

____

____

____

____

____

A family is a place where principles are hammered and honed on the anvil of everyday living.

CHARLES SWINDOLL

Vacation Highlights

One of the best trips our family ever took was:

The first time you traveled by yourself, I felt:

Some of my favorite vacation memories are:

You Put a Smile in My Heart

— My Favorite Photos of You

PLACE PHOTO HERE

The happiest moments of my life have been the few which I have passed at home in the bosom of my family.

THOMAS JEFFERSON

PLACE PHOTO HERE

All Grown Up

Your personality is: ______________________________

____

Things that make you laugh: ______________________________

____

You're a big softie when it comes to: ______________________________

____

____

Your hardest struggle has been: ______________________________

____

____

You're naturally good at: ______________________________

____

____

You have very strong opinions about: ______________________________

____

____

____

____

PLACE PHOTO HERE

The Love of Your Life

When you first met the love of your life, I felt: ___________________

____

____

____

____

When you told me you were getting married, I thought: ___________

____

____

____

____

____

On your wedding day, I hoped: ___________

____

____

____

____

____

____

What I love most about the person you married:

If I could have one wish for your marriage, it would be:

Private Thoughts from Mom

The guiding values and beliefs in my life are:

The hardest thing I've ever had to do was:

One of the happiest moments of my life was when:

My philosophy of life is:

If I could live one part of my life over again, I might:

If I could change one aspect of being a mother to you, I:

Motherhood is the greatest potential influence in human society. Her caress first awakens in the child a sense of security; her kiss the first realization of affection; her sympathy and tenderness, the first assurance that there is love in the world.

DAVID MCKAY

From My Heart to Yours

You mean so much to me because: ___

How having you has changed my life: ___

Being your mother has taught me: ___

I have never felt closer to you than when: ___

I am so proud of the way you: ________________________________

I have always admired your: ____________________

I've never told you this, but: ________________________________

I would like my grandkids to know that you: ____________________

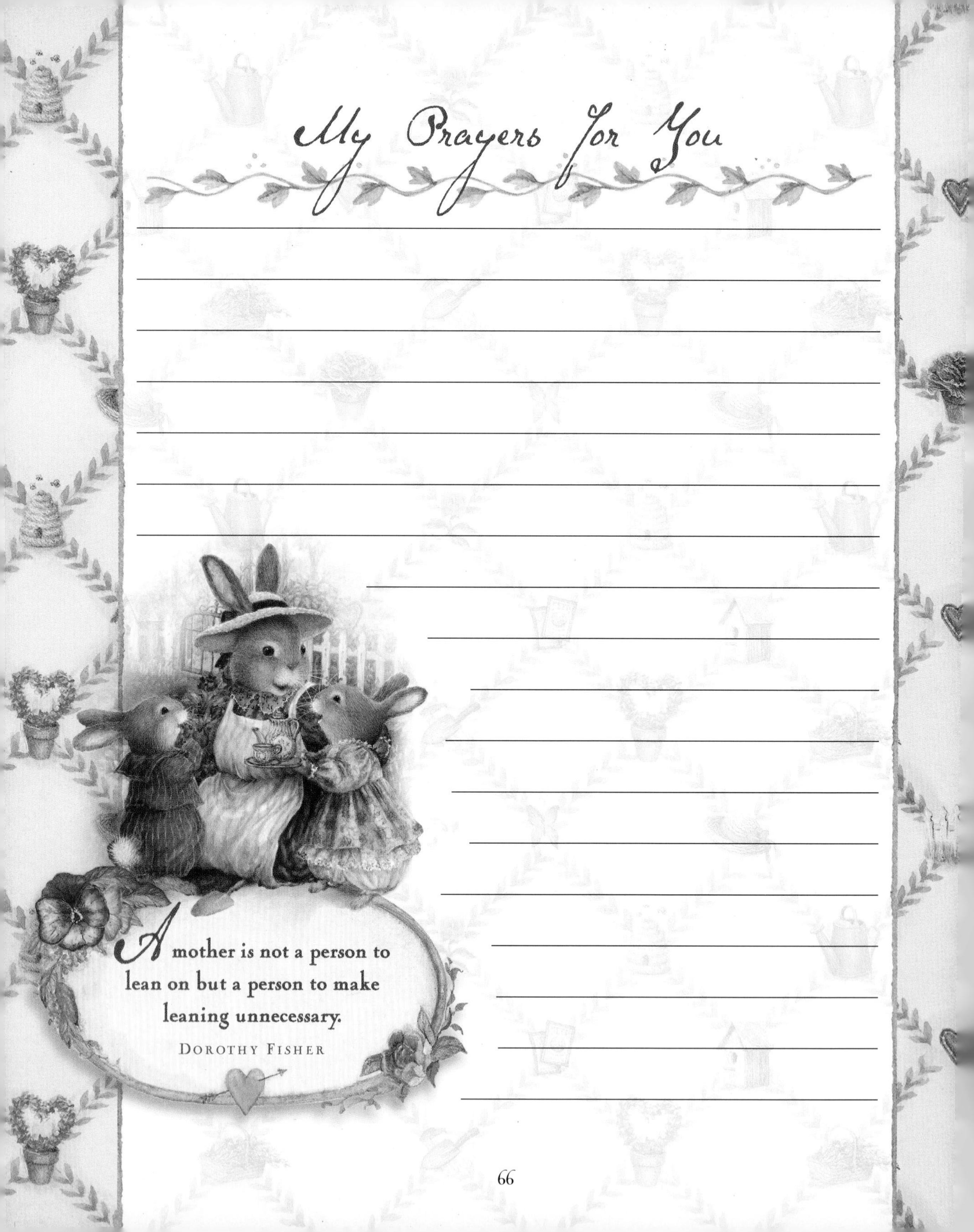

My Prayers for You

A mother is not a person to lean on but a person to make leaning unnecessary.

DOROTHY FISHER

Other Sweet Sentiments

Treasured Keepsakes

Place Mementos Here

Little one, you're such a small person in such a great big world. But God shows His power in all that He has made and His love in caring for every little thing.

TWILA PARIS

PLACE MEMENTOS HERE

Place Mementos Here

Place Mementos Here

PLACE MEMENTOS HERE

Place Mementos Here

Place Mementos Here

Place Mementos Here

Everybody says I look just like my mother.
Everybody says I'm the image of Aunt Bee.
Everybody says my nose is like my father's,
But I want to look like me.

Dorothy Aldis

Dear Child of Mine

May your father
and mother be glad;
may she who gave
you birth rejoice!

THE BOOK OF PROVERBS